Simply Stated

Simply Stated

Tononiya D.

authorHOUSE®

AuthorHouse™ LLC
1663 Liberty Drive
Bloomington, IN 47403
www.authorhouse.com
Phone: 1-800-839-8640

Published by AuthorHouse 11/15/2013

ISBN: 978-1-4918-3556-2 (sc)
ISBN: 978-1-4918-3557-9 (e)

Library of Congress Control Number: 2013921171

THE POWER OF LIFE OR DEATH
LAY ON YOUR TONGUE

Contents

"It's not the title of a relationship that makes it a relationship but the love of the people that exist in it!"

I Wanna Get Lost With You

I wanna get lost with you

I wanna get lost with you

I wanna get lost with you

I wanna get lost

I wanna be blindfolded and led into the center of clones unknown and see if your eyes will be my sight

I wanna get lost with you

I wanna get lost with you

I wanna get lost with you

I wanna get lost

I wanna get lost like first time hikers confused by the sun and the moon and fear not the sounds that come along with the night

I wanna get lost with you

I wanna get lost with you

I wanna get lost with you

I wanna get lost

I want our souls to get lost like the clouds and the sky and not know where you or I begin or end like our skin intertwined

And

I

I wanna get lost with you

I wanna get lost with you

I wanna get lost with you

I wanna get lost

I wanna ride off sounds silenced by time embraced by love and loving its breeze on our face as we face the next curve in line with each other

I wanna get lost with you

I wanna get lost with you

I wanna get lost with you

I wanna get lost

I wanna get lost with you like logic does when you're climbing the high of ecstasy and your destiny is to climax so you don't feel the intensity of the nails digging in your back 'til you're in the show and they start to sting

I wanna get lost with you

I wanna get lost with you

I wanna get lost with you

I wanna get lost

I wanna walk in your shoes and see if you can feel each step
I take in place of you, the way I feel you, when you take them
for me, for we

I wanna get lost with you

I wanna get lost with you

I wanna get lost with you

I wanna get lost

I wanna melt in your skin so I know what it feels like to cover
you, then weep as I detach.

I wanna get lost with you

I wanna get lost with you

I wanna get lost with you

I wanna get lost

I wanna drown in the thoughts of your love and have its
reality revive me

I wanna get lost with you

I wanna get lost with you

I wanna get lost with you

I wanna get lost

I wanna exist close enough to you that I inhale deep, your
fears and you exhale bold fearlessness

I wanna get lost with you

I wanna get lost with you

I wanna get lost with you

I wanna get lost

See

I want to say the words

I

Love

You

And hear their reflection

Sometimes

Sometimes

I kiss you in your sleep

I let my lips embrace your skin

Melt into you soft and slow

Connect as a whole

For a moment before I ease them away

If only for a moment they were a perfect match

And the blind was a mix beautifully combined

Sometimes

I kiss you in your sleep

Soft

Smooth

With both our eyes closed

Yours covering your dreams

Mine

Ignite a dreamlike state

Two Way

I think of love, love

You love, huh, when

Cause I love

Tough, smile love

Times get tough

Praise even when

Thanks not enough

Enough to have you

Loved, loves me

Blessed by Jesus, GOD

Me from heaven or

From heaven, sent

Love, loving you

Love, unconditional is

Love is you, unconditional

I smile, cause I love,

When I think of love

*Now read upwards; last sentence first . . .

Words and I

I took her for granted and almost lost her

But she is a part of me that I cannot be without

I can't breathe without

Because she is my air

And without her I am lifeless

So I stand and face her need to have

All

Of

Me

And I embrace her intensely

Because I have come to love her

As deep if not deeper than

I love poetry

So she makes me work for her

And

Work I do

'Til daybreak through sun rise

Exposing my need for her

And

She gives me another chance to

Indulge in her essence

And I will never

Make

Her

Feel

Unappreciated

Again

Anticipation

Anticipated, anticipation, intensified

Through times of turmoil and self-doubt you stood true

Never a letdown, slip up, or displace of affection, your heart, smile, soul comfort shined through warming the chilled core of me

So it's a given

When lit by lights higher prevail it will be the name you were given that I will yell

In variables of love, laughter, and positive security

Countless as the times beneath the moon I've watch your humility until the sun's set releasing my soul to your captivity far beyond the depth of your sexuality

That has me speaking words of poetry

Soundless

After years still heard in its entirety

As I examine your tone honey dipped in intoxicating exoticism that keeps my loyalty straight in the midst of dazed illusions

Where many hoped I'd fail and change the course of what I know to be fate

The path less traveled

Unfamiliar now familiar

The taste of pleasure divine

Anticipated, anticipation, intensified

In every way imaginable and my imagination is just what it is

So I dance with its ideas

Because I love the shit it reveals

Like the ocean being lit by an eclipse's edge that hasn't been covered yet and we make it onto the wave beaten sand that supports our feet as we become complete

Witnessed by nature and its creatures

Then darkness

To awake with the light of the sun

u

When I look at you I hear soft tone melodies like Music Soul Childs <u>Don't Change, Ribbons in the sky,</u> <u>All for you</u>, <u>Whenever wherever whatever</u> and of course the words that keep our minds, bodies, and souls together <u>Always and forever</u> and I think that's how I want each moment shared with you If somehow time has not allowed you to see just how good your love is to me I'm going to let you know You are the la lo medic melody that calms the rhythmic beat of my heart Though some don't understand I am still here with the strength of my love that will forever hold your hand So follow the rhythmical beat of my left breast and with its thumb let your stress or pain fade Cause my love, the love I have for you will always remain

<u>To my lover and soul mate for life</u>

"The blessing in your fall is not just in getting up but being able to see the people closest to you from a different angle."

Kept

My soul is spiraling

My heart's at a stand still

Everything in my mind's telling me to walk away

But my love makes me stay still

And the chills trail the heated flesh that's left

The heated flesh that's left behind

Distant memories

Different fantasies

Tainted reality of lies that merge into false truths that

Code, cushion, and sustain

Each look

Each tear

Each glare that breaks through walls

Hardened, softened, hardened, then softened

By bloodlines that tide together

Like streams to rivers

And

Emotions flow opposite of life's path designed

Or designed too complex for one to follow

How hollow is the pain in this black hole

Filled in darkness

Emptied through beams of light, sound, weeps, and screams

And my dreams

Make me a dreamer

So I hope that I never wake

Because

Truth's clear

Everyone cares for more than self

And there is no need for help

So I erase the word from existence

And resistance submits to unity

Between you and me

Not just in the communities

But as a nation

And patience has haste for better days

Where

I love you

Is spoken not abbreviated

Luv

On our laptops and computer screens

And my breath has wings stronger than the links in the chains that once held us down

But

Here I am

On my knees

So crawl into me and I will keep us afloat

Free

And kept without hands

Belief

You tell me that you love me and I believe you

I believe the look in your eyes

The tone in your voice

The intensity in your touch

When I feel you touch me

And as long as you embrace me

And your lips are making me want to feel them all over me till I fall asleep underneath their softness

You tell me you love me and I believe you

Every time you say it

As often as you say it

You tell me you love me and I believe you

Because

I have nothing to compare it to

I Wish

I wish I could scream loud enough to compensate for all the times I couldn't speak

I wish I could punch holes in the concrete walls I placed around my heart to lessen the vibration of its aching beat

I wish I could stand firmer but I have to shift the weight off of my blistering feet

I wish I could cleanse my soul with my own tears

I wish I could go back to the times when I simply wished you were here, but I can't have that you without giving up my search for me

I wish that make believe could make me believe in fairytales unseen

I wish that sight was silent and that pain really did set you free

I wish that wishes really came true, so that I could wish my love strong enough to forgive you

Rainbow

Two bodies one and the same

On sands of time laying intertwined
nakedly without shame

Only pride

From being washed, yet surviving life's rain

Then dried in chains of

Red red red red red red

Orange orange orange orange orange orange

Yellow yellow yellow yellow yellow yellow

Green green green green green green

Blue blue blue blue blue blue

Purple purple purple purple purple purple

Deep

That forms a rainbow of two souls now complete

We've Become

How distant we've become

Once long lost pieces that fit each curve

And defined every line that laced the seams that

formulate into me

Your smile

I miss more each day

But less than

The miss of the smile that you placed on mine

How distant we've become

Why

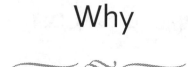

Why couldn't I have laid upon your chest and find comfort from the beat in the left side of your breast? Then rest the fear of the unknown and love long gone away in your arms. Instead the screams clashed with its own sounds and effects. As you take away my true pleasure of touch. And not only define love but the relationship between pleasure and such touch inappropriately.

"People only show you what they want you to see but if you look closely you will see them in their entirety!"

<u>Blue Skies</u>

In the absence of your touch

Silence no longer remains

And the strain of rain to fall and blend with my

tears

Cries out in liquid screams

While my soul dances in darkness

So no one can see its uncontrolled rhyme
and make a mockery of its freed state

Replaced by lit night

That covers day

Or gray skies

Through

Blue.

DNA

What have I done to you? What have you done to me?
If actions can tear down ones soul then let them tear
down both the houses dismissal and protectant that
you and I live in. Let the broken pieces shatter and hit
the ground. Loosen the world wind grip that strangles
me. Let me gasp until my breathing stabilizes and this
house is strong enough to be a home without walls and
both of us can finally see that we share the same DNA.

Truth Is

Truth is

I am hurt by the realities of truth so my heart squeezes then it must release

Piece by piece

Shame bit by shame bit

I let it hit the inside of my brain and project images that create sight

Flash by flash

Laugh by laugh

The imprints are stronger than the existence is, was, or ever will be again

And I've swam in sorrow for tomorrow and my yesterday for

far too long now

Now I'm hurt by reality's truth

So my heart squeezes and must release

And though there isn't much of me

Or

I should say not enough of me to save you

I gave you all of me

And somehow reality's truth is

You

Could

Care

Less

"*When dealing with people the uncertainty doesn't lie in whether or not they can hurt you but rather in the questioning of if they can truly love and nurture you!*"

Clenched Fist

Clenched fist

Open hand

Echoed screams cling to sound waves as they ripple
through the air

Broken promises

Cover me

Pounding blows against my skin demand to seep into my
flesh and remove all the hope that is left in me like they
removed the good intentions once in you

Clenched fist

Open hand

Rage unleashed like a pit in a pit and you fight my love to
the death

And you

Fight love to death

With no remorse you inhale its last breath with a

Clenched fist

And I succumb with a

Open hand

You Ask

The water is running and I'm naked and wet

Yet you ask me what I need

See, you feed my body and yet you leave my soul longing to know what it feels like to be full

So if I lather my sin with your words will their actions cleanse me or leave me dirty

Like my loves past

The water is running and I'm naked and wet

Yet you ask me what it is that I need

And my eyes plead for you to see for yourself that I'm naked showing you all the scars that I use to cover with baggy pants and a smile

My eyes

Plead

For you to hear the laughter that's full of innocence

Like when I was a child

Pure and untainted

That

I

Laugh

For

You

The water is running and I'm naked and wet

Yet you ask me what it is that I need

Only

Because I have become the picture that you have painted

of me

So you fulfill only her needs

I

Guess I'm worth a thousand words to you

But I can't seem to choose the right

One

Because my heart doesn't speak the English language

Nor does it speak the dialect that you originate from

So there is

Silence

Silence that meets silence head on like vibrating waves of sound

Useless

The water is running and I'm naked and wet

And you ask me what it is that I really need

Know You

Through your armor I hear your voice and in your eyes truth peeks through. And it makes me think, feel, I want to get to know you. I mean get to know you beyond the guard once needed to protect your essence this lessened state of communication has me speechless . . . and each list of beautiful things turned grotesque began to fade until Emotions form and your laughter's echo causes the strange of painless days to fall down like rain . . . but unlike the rain that I seek to wash me it's iced and I'm winter cold to your warmth safely sheltered in someone else's name . . .

Through your armor I hear your voice and in your eyes truth peeks through.

And I see that your censored love wants to be true, true to love . . . but love in you is so hard to do . . .

I Love You

I love u's are always lies formulated in the moment

In the moment of truth exposed that try to escape as soon as its clarity is seen

I love you

More like I love that you can't see me in all my shades of darkness that once set bold in the light of some one's eyes that I once longed to love me

I love you

The concept of love undefined because I never knew love

Because it was never defined

Felt

Or shown to me but I love

Innocent eyes looking at my surface not ashamed to hold

on to my soul

Damaged

Before I ever knew it even belonged to me

I love you

Tononiya D.

In your daughters eyes

In your daughters eyes

Lays the lives of our nation

Lays the lies of a misdefined definition of reproduction

Or reproducing life

Reproducing mistakes of yours

And aged mothers many times prior to this moment

This time

In her eyes

Cries the need to drown out the noise
of your silent chaotic feed

That you stream continuously into her
from an uncut umbilical cord

"Knowing who you are and making others address you as such are two very different things."

I am

I am the memory of the melody "I believe the
children are the future, teach them well and let
them lead the way. Show them all the beauty
they possess inside." On a clear and

sunny day

I am the wooden chest of secret horrors of
inappropriate touch, sexual and physical and all of the
lies, fears, and intimidation needed to keep it sealed

I am a child nurtured

I am a child unloved

I am a voiceless coward, curled in a corner
covered in darkness with my eyes looking up
at the street light praying for the dark night
to quickly change to the light of day

I am silent screams turned into reoccurring nightmares

I am bending rage that prays to love to love me

I am anger that can only be measured by peace

I am an addict to each level of my ancestry
so I willingly smack my arm clench my fist
and make my vain accessible for use

I am a sense of pride

*I am old strength like old money it never
ends, so I give it to all that need it*

*I am courage so I bravely fight for
those who have not found theirs*

I am honest because I know the pain of a lie to well

*I am an advocate because I know somewhere
out there someone needs me*

I am

Laughter

Free

Joyous

And uplifting

*I am the dawn of a new day, filled
with infinite possibilities*

Morning

I open my eyes

Slide one leg to the edge of the bed then the other

Sit up

Slip one foot into my house shoes and do the same to the other

I take a few steps and

I think of you

Pause

Continue

Click the light on in the bathroom

Grab my solution

Put my contacts in, right then left

Look at your reflection

With solution trails like tears

I think of you

Touch my lips

Try to remember your smile because I don't think it's the same

I run the water

Brush my teeth

Wash my face

I think of you

Take one last look in the mirror

See who I've become

I miss you

Turn out the light

Breathe softly

Prepare myself for the next step that I have to take without you

Seed

On my way to pick up my sight I am enlightened

I am informed that I am the image of my mother

And not just in vision but in DNA

DNA of which is in twins

But I am the seed

I am the seed of a soul that loved freely

I am the seed of a soul that had to be the man to prove he could stroke a woman back to a world of social normalcy

Now I see why self-contradiction resides in me

All so loving and arrogant in the same breath

So why didn't anyone tell me?

Why didn't you fucking tell me?

I have the right to know

Don't you see?

Can't you see?

That by knowing her

I get to know and understand my own identity

Define what's destined in me

Yet you disguise the truth

To create the feminine woman that's right for you

In me

And the more you do

Her soul speaks louder through me

Because she is me and unfortunately

I am you too

Two individuals

Intertwined

Unspoken

Unseen

Unknown still felt

The hair you admired

Gone

The eyes you weakened

Clear in focus

The lips you long to press yours against

Speak out truth that your ears cannot withstand

The heart broken

It loves with each beat despite what may come and what it has been through

And my hands

Record time to paper making these things timeless

Shared

Shared

Ice cream from a melting cone you shared through a smile and laughter

A skate from your pair

Half of your Pink Panther seat so we both could feel the wind on our faces at the same time

Colecovision and a joy stick that was never mine

That came from a father you called our very own

To protect me from the pain of knowing my young eyes had not laid sight on my father after the beating our brothers put on his ass

After they couldn't take him wailing on them and mom anymore

Half the profits of the front yard mango sales because they made us rich

The pink side of the box of nerds

While you took the green

The hands

Lips

Words

Acts of betrayal

From a man who was supposed to protect us but traveled a forbidden course

So, you took over his job and sacrificed your joy to guard mine

Yeah, you took the green nerds and in their consumption consumed the rest of your childhood

Mother and the one thing you thought it all worth

Me

As a result began the secret pain silenced by man formed beast

Until time escape brought forth anew

Harnessed tears and emotions for years without you

Reunited, release, shared

Children as though they were conceived by the strength of our love alone

Shared acceptance through a smile and laughter as we eat

Ice cream from a melting cone

"Royalty can be obtained but it cannot be erased."

Comfort in my discomfort

My loss hoped for

No

Prayed for like

Rain in a drought of withering beauty
in danger of the wind

Prayed for

Your gain of leverage that I might
remain the same as you do

That I remain the same as you

Cloned

With each step taken that of the original before you

Proof that life is brutal and I am slain by its volatile attack

From the front, back, left, and the right

Right . . .

I still breathe life

Frozen

Then shattered by this burning freeze

In this breeze I am naked

I

Am

Naked

Yet something still covers me

Hovers above me

See

Might I dance through the faces of Satan's helpers

Familiar they seem

And land hand and hand in the center of its clan

Shaved by blades like the one I shave
my own face with daily

And

I

Begin

To

Waltz

I begin to waltz with this two-horned one-
tailed demonic illusion unmasked

I begin to waltz with this demonic illusion unmasked

And it's glance of fire strikes ablaze around
us as to cause a daze filled maze

That my soul becomes trapped in

My ambitions, desires, my own fuel-filled fires

Wrapped

In

Like this spin of trickery

That has yet to get to me

Its lips send to me invitations rejected times before

Pleads

Pleads to adore

To adore it

As

It

Adores

Me

Deceitfully

Then faceless faces look up to me through peeling flesh

At best

This is what's left after all your worldly
dreams have been given to you

I laugh through my smile laced words

My

Soul

Is

His

Soul

And the floors drop

Into a pitted flame and shame clears the air

I am here

But

Where are you

You were bold and antagonistic through fallacies

Yet you run from truth

Then a door slams

And

A voice says

Hell cannot use you

If I were a poet

If I were a poet I would make an instrumental melody with my vocabulary

I would let the hook be the repetition of exclamation marks in between the verbal collage of my life's memories

If I were a poet

I would let each poem self-select and auto play based on the emotions of the day and sway my mood whichever way it desired until I desired more

As long as I desired more from this life, and the pleasures in it.

If I were a poet

I would create a master piece with letters perfectly synchronized to reveal the hidden truth, lies and injustices that keeps our minds rested and the fallacies untested so that they can no longer continue to be passed down from generation to generation like a heritage that is funded by welfare and iron bars impatiently awaited to be received because our history is only supposed to be as deep as slavery and even then freedom was given not taken

If I were a poet

I would engrave Zulu and Nyabinghi in the place of our ancestor's strength and African decent and its dismissal, this misdefinition of color unprotested like time unchanged just rearranged to display itself differently

If I were a poet

I would write words so close and continuous that at first sight they appear to be jumbled rhetoric until closer examination like Egyptian hieroglyphics deciphered

If I were a poet

I would use a multitude of reasons transformed into meanings exposed through tone to evaluate and elevate the minds and souls of those within reach, that I might reach them

If I were a poet

I would write a poem with my face east

Facing the sun and my back to the moon in hopes that a new sunrise is never too late and turning my back on past days is never too soon

If

I

Were

A

Poet

"Love does not come with a limit, people do."

Coward

"Fucking coward" I spit till I bleed words of truth by the hour and your time is coming soon indeed. I've been taught that revenge is not mine but the LORDS and I know that GOD sees and hears my begs and pleads. Not only for his wrath to rock but destroy your being from its core. I pray in tears out front of your door ready to split your shit and become your punisher and dissolve your shell quick to let you feel the hand that the woman you're fucking up's genetically bonded with because you want it the way you give it. Your words through her lips. Secretly controlled each hit you gave that I didn't know but I am aware of all of it. But it is GOD who has kept you safe from annihilation bitter for you sweet for me. Damn I want to split your shit brother you better give thanks to the GOD in me. Yet the word says do on to others as you would have them do on to you. So I can take that piece and run with it like half of these hypocritical Christians do. And hunt you like the prey you are . . . You "Fucking Coward"

*"People enter your life for a reason,
season, or a lifetime . . . and I thank GOD
for all of the lessons learned . . ."*

Daringly

Bold and joyously I look at you

Unafraid of your soul's history or even its present state

And I smile at the thought of learning lessons of journeys
untraveled and knowledge of those past my age

In this place

Space

Time

I daringly await you

Moments

Can you believe the moment of love, being in love with you . . . was when we ran to get away from the rain in separate paths to end on the same journey. I said to come in from a journeyed path the same, pain, stained, fairy tales . . . as rails of a crippled child's dreams . . . gleams be for reality's intrusion. Making past memories from present moments growing eager to age into the future with you to see if the sparkle in your eye intensifies with the days and the ways you love, we love, I am cripple no more my mind like that of a child with endless possibilities of super hero's with invisible identities that rise with me and I it.

How do I

How do I share desire, passion, lust, the hunger for your spirits cream, dreams, and aspirations

How do I deal with the thought of others fingers tracing the exterior of smooth caramel that counsels your soul

How do I deal with the seduction of your enlightened brown eyes, captured in an unframed portrait for others to see

The answer is simple

With the knowledge that

You were beautifully created to shine

Pieces of me

Yesterday has come and gone like the moment turned
into opportunity, and the opportunity turned to chance,
then that chance turned into memories of faded smiles of
each and every one of you that I remember still . . .

*"To find yourself means that you lost
yourself at some point!"*

*Poetry will always be the light that helpsme
find my way through the darkness.*